I0554909

LIVING IN GOD'S WORLD
A Book of Instruction
for Children of All Ages

By Pamela A. James, B.R.E.

Mill Lake Books

Copyright © 2023 by Pamela A. James
No part of this book may be reproduced in any form without written permission, except for brief quotations in critical reviews.

Scripture quotations are taken from *Holy Bible*, New Living Translation, copyright © 1996, 2004, 2015 by Tyndale House Foundation. Used by permission of Tyndale House Publishers, Inc., Carol Stream, Illinois 60188. All rights reserved.

Illustrations were drawn by and are the property of Pamela A. James.

Cover design by Pamela A. James and Dean Tjepkema

Published by Mill Lake Books
Chilliwack, BC
Canada
jamescoggins.wordpress.com/mill-lake-books

Printed by Lightning Source, distributed by Ingram

ISBN: 978-1-998787-02-9

Topics covered in this book

Where did our world come from?
How did it get here?

Did you ever look up at the night sky with all its stars, and wonder how they got there? Have you ever wondered how a beautiful shell you found on the beach got its shape, or how a rock you picked up got its beautiful colors? Have you ever wondered who designed them and put them here? The answer is that God designed them and put them here. He made the whole world in just six days...the fish in the sea, the birds in the sky, the animals and people on earth, the flowers and trees, and the rocks and shells too. He made them all! Then, He had everything He had done written down in His special book, the Holy Bible. Here is what the Bible says:

"In the beginning, God created the heavens and the earth." (Genesis 1:1)

"The Lord merely spoke, and the heavens were created...and all the stars were born. He assigned the sea its boundaries and locked the oceans in vast reservoirs." (Psalm 33:6,7)

"God created everything...and nothing was created except through him."
(John 1:3)

"For the Lord is the one who shaped the mountains." (Amos 4:13)

Why should I learn about God?

Let's start with this reason: You are living in a world that God made. And it isn't only the seashells and rocks that He made. He made you, too. And not only did God make you, but He also loves you! He knows every detail about you. He knows what you are thinking and what you say and do. He even knows what is ahead for you in your life. Wouldn't you want to know someone like that? Wouldn't you want to love Him as much as He loves you?

Here is what the Bible says:

"Acknowledge that the Lord is God! He made us, and we are his." (Psalm 100:3)

"The very hairs on your head are all numbered." (Luke 12:7)

"You care for people…O Lord. How precious is your unfailing love, O God." (Psalm 36:6-7)

"You…know everything about me. You know when I sit down or stand up. You know my thoughts even when I'm far away…You know what I am going to say before I say it, Lord…You saw me before I was born. Every day of my life was recorded in your book. Every moment was laid out before a single day had passed." (Psalm 139:1,2,4,16)

What does God want me to do?

The first thing God wants you to do, since He loves you and cares about you so much, is to love him back.

He says in the Bible:

"You must love the Lord your God with all your heart, all your soul, and all your strength." *(Deuteronomy 6:5)*

How can you do that? By obeying the rules He set down in the Bible for everyone who lives in His world. In the Bible, He says:

"If you love me, obey my commandments…All who love Me will do what I say." (John 14:15,23)

What are the "Commandments"? They are God's rules for living in His world, rules for us to obey so that we can all live together in a way that makes God happy He made us. Let's look at some of God's Commandments that He set down in the Bible…

Here are some of the "Commandments" (rules for living) that God has given us in His Bible:

"You must not have any other god but me." (Exodus 20:3)

"You must not misuse the name of the Lord your God." (Exodus 20:7)

"Remember to observe the Sabbath day by keeping it holy." (Exodus 20:8)

"Honor your father and mother." (Exodus 20:12)

"You must not murder... You must not steal... You must not testify falsely against your neighbor." (Exodus 20:13-16)

"Never seek revenge or bear a grudge...but love your neighbor as yourself." (Leviticus 19:18)

As you go through life, there will be times when you have a decision to make about which way you will go or which thing you will do. If you remember God's Commandments and other advice he has put in the Bible and do your best to obey Him, God will help you choose the right way to go and the right thing to do.

There is good advice in other parts of the Bible as well. Let's think about times when you have to choose how you will respond to a situation, and let's see what the Bible says about it...

Why do I have to obey my parents?
I can't stand all the rules
they expect me to follow.
Why can't I just live
the way I want to?

Here is what the Bible says:

"My child, listen when your father corrects you. Don't neglect your mother's instruction. What you learn from them will crown you with grace and be a chain of honor around your neck." (Proverbs 1:8-9)

"A wise child accepts a parent's discipline." (Proverbs 13:1)

"Honor your father and mother." (Exodus 20:12)

"Children, always obey your parents, for this pleases the Lord." (Colossians 3:20)

"Only a fool despises a parent's discipline; whoever learns from correction is wise." (Proverbs 15:5)

God knows that your parents have learned many lessons in their lives, not only from the things their parents taught them, but also from the experiences of living day by day, experiences you have yet to face. Your parents have been in this world much longer than you! God wants you to listen to them, not so that they can boss you around, but so that you will grow up to be wise and honorable, becoming the person God wants you to be.

Why do I have to go to church?
There are so many other things I'd rather be doing
with my friends than
going to church!
It's a day off from school!

Here is what the Bible says:

*"Remember to observe the
Sabbath day by keeping it holy.
You have six days a week for your
ordinary work, but the seventh
day is a Sabbath day of rest
dedicated to the Lord your God."*
(Exodus 20:8-10)

"Let us not neglect our meeting together.
(Hebrews 10:25)

*"Give to the Lord the glory He deserves! Bring your
offering and come into his presence."*
(1 Chronicles 16:29)

God is clearly telling us that we should set aside one day a week as holy to
Him. He is inviting you to spend that day with him and with other people
who love Him. That's not too much to ask. After all, think of all He has done
for you. He provides for all your needs, loves you and takes care of you, and
has made a place in Heaven for you where you can live with Him forever.
So, doesn't He deserve your attention? Take time to praise and thank Him
and bring an offering to Him.

Why is it so wrong to tell a lie?
Do I have to be honest all the time?

Here is what the Bible says:

"Truth stands the test of time, but lies are soon exposed." (Proverbs 12:19)

"Don't lie to each other." (Colossians 3:9)

"The Lord detests lying lips, but he delights in those who tell the truth." (Proverbs 12:22)

"A lying tongue hates its victims, and flattering words cause ruin." (Proverbs 26:28)

What does all this mean? When you lie, there are consequences. In time, your lie will be discovered and may bring you trouble. God hates it when you lie. Do you really want to disappoint Him? When you lie to other people, you show them that you don't really value their friendship because you aren't being honest with them. In time, if you continue to lie, people will begin to mistrust you. Stop and

think about it before you tell a lie. And if you have told one, ask the Lord to forgive you and then go to the person to whom you have lied and ask for that person's forgiveness.

Why do people make such a fuss about it when I get angry?
Okay, I admit it! Sometimes people make me so mad I lose my cool and start shouting at them or pushing them, but they deserve it!

Here is what the Bible says:

"Better to be patient than powerful."
(Proverbs 16:32)

"People with understanding control their anger; a hot temper shows great foolishness."
(Proverbs 14:29)

"Don't sin by letting anger control you…for anger gives a foothold to the devil."
(Ephesians 4:26-27)

Satan, also called the Devil in the Bible, is God's enemy. He is always looking for ways to trip up those who are trying to obey God. He loves it when one of God's children loses his temper, because losing your temper can cause you to make mistakes, such as saying things you don't mean or doing things you shouldn't do. Losing your temper makes you forget the wisdom God has given you, and it makes God very sad to see this. He wants you to learn that controlling your temper is even better than having great physical strength.

What am I supposed to do when people do mean things to me?
I hate my brother for losing my favorite book! I am going to think of some way I can get back at him so he will never touch my stuff again.

Here is what the Bible says:

"Don't say, 'I will get even for this wrong.' Wait for the Lord to handle the matter." (Proverbs 20:22)

"Do not nurse hatred in your heart for any of your relatives." (Leviticus 19:17)

"Never pay back evil with more evil...Do all that you can to live in peace with everyone... 'I will take revenge, I will pay them back,' says the Lord." (Romans 12:17-19)

It's not your job to punish people for their sins. That's God's job. You are not permitted by God to get even with anybody. You are commanded to love everybody, including your family members! Instead of plotting to get even, ask God to help your brother be more careful with other people's things.

Why do I have to give?

Mom says I should give away some of my clothes because I have too many. I don't think I have too many! I want to keep them all! Just because I have more things than some poor people, why is it my job to give stuff to them? Let someone else do it!

Here is what the Bible says:

"God loves a person who gives cheerfully. And God will generously provide all you need. Then you will always have everything you need and plenty left over to share with others."
(2 Corinthians 9:7-8)

"What good is it…if you say you have faith but don't prove it by your actions?…Suppose you see a brother or a sister who has no food or clothing and…you don't give that person any food or clothing. What good does that do?…Faith by itself isn't enough. Unless it produces good deeds, it is dead and useless." (James 2:14-17)

You cannot claim to be a follower of God and not care about the needs of others. God is not pleased with those who have no compassion for the poor. After all, He has given you everything you own, and He has promised that if you share, and do it without grumbling, He will provide for all your needs, and you will always have enough for yourself and some to share with others.

Why is this world so full of rules?
There are rules everywhere I go…
"No Trespassing", "Don't
Walk", "Don't litter."
Why should I have to obey these
rules people make?
Life would be so much more
fun without them!

Here is what the Bible says:

"Submit to the government and its officers…Be obedient, always ready to do what is good." (Titus 3:1)

"Submit to governing authorities. For all authority comes from God…So anyone who rebels against authority is rebelling against what God has instituted, and they will be punished….Do what is right, and they will honor you. The authorities are God's servants, sent for your good. But if you are doing wrong, of course you should be afraid, for they have the power to punish you." (Romans 13:1-4)

Laws are put in place to help people live an orderly, peaceful life. Policemen are there to help you when you have problems, but if you break the law, it is their job to bring you to the authorities for punishment. God wants you to obey the rules and to show respect for those whose job it is to enforce them. God has commanded us to love our neighbors too, which means not going uninvited (trespassing) on their property or littering the sidewalks and parks which they enjoy. All these rules are for the good of everyone, including you.

Why do I have to keep my promises?
Mom gets so upset with me
if I say I will clean my room
and then don't do it.
What's all the fuss about?
After all, I'm just a kid.
Does it really matter
if I don't keep my promises?

Here is what the Bible says:

"The Lord detests lying lips, but he delights in those who tell the truth." (Proverbs 12:22)

"Even children are known by the way they act, whether their conduct is pure, and whether it is right." (Proverbs 20:11)

"The Lord always keeps his promises; he is gracious in all he does." (Psalm 145:13)

"Choose a good reputation over great riches; being held in high esteem is better than silver or gold." (Proverbs 22:1)

God always keeps His promises…can you imagine what it would be like for us if He didn't? You may think people don't notice when you break a promise, but they do. And if breaking your promises becomes a habit for you, no one will believe you when you say you will do something. You will have an untrustworthy reputation which will be difficult to repair. Keeping your promises, having the trust of others, is more valuable than having lots of money.

Do I have to avoid entertainment that contains violence or profanity? I watched a video that had a whole lot of swear words and violence in it. But it was a really good story. I think that made up for all the other stuff. Most good movies have swear words and sometimes violence in them. When you turn on the TV, you hear it there, too. It's hard to get away from it! What does God think about it? He's not against my getting some entertainment, is He?

Here is what the Bible says:

"A wise person is hungry for knowledge, while the fool feeds on trash." (Proverbs 15:14)

"Fix your thoughts on what is true, and honorable, and right, and pure, and lovely, and admirable…things that are excellent and worthy of praise." (Philippians 4:8)

In his lifetime, Israel's most beloved king, David, tried to please God every day, and he made God this promise, which we should too if we love God and want to obey Him:

"I will be careful to live a blameless life…I will live a life of integrity in my own home. I will refuse to look at anything vile and vulgar." (Psalm 101:2-3)

Why does it matter who my friends are?

Mom and Dad are always telling me to be careful who I hang around with at school. Why is that so important? Doesn't God want me to be friendly with everyone? Some of those guys my parents call "rebels" are very popular at school. Yeah, maybe they get into more trouble than average, but if I hang around with them, I'll have lots of friends.

Here is what the Bible says:

"Walk with the wise and become wise; associate with fools and get in trouble." Proverbs 13:20)

"If the godly give in to the wicked, it is like polluting a fountain or muddying a spring." (Proverbs 25:26)

"My child, fear the Lord…Don't associate with rebels, for disaster will hit them suddenly." (Proverbs 24:21-22.)

"The godly give good advice to their friends; the wicked lead them astray." (Proverbs 12:26)

You may think that if you spend your time with a person who laughs at rules, or is mean, or uses foul language, you can be a good influence on that person. That may be possible, but it is more likely that this person will lead you into doing things God doesn't want you to do. Also, by siding with that person, you are saying that you approve of that person's behavior. Think about it! Choose your friends carefully.

What does it mean to trust God?
The Bible says that God
made me and loves me.
Well, sometimes things in my world
make me worried or scared.
I worry that I won't have
enough food to eat,
or I get scared that
something might happen to me.
What should I do when I
get worried or scared?

Here is what the Bible says:

"Give all your worries and cares to God, for he cares about you." (1 Peter 5:7)

"The Lord is a shelter for the oppressed, a refuge in times of trouble. Those who know your name trust in you, for You, O Lord, do not abandon those who search for You." (Psalm 9:9-10)

"I tell you not to worry about everyday life—whether you have enough food and drink, or enough clothes to wear…your heavenly Father already knows all your needs…and he will give you everything you need."
(Matthew 6:25,32-33)

Just ask the Lord for whatever you need, and if you are faithful to Him, He will provide for you. And whenever you are afraid, whether it be of people or things happening today or what might happen tomorrow, you can rely on your Heavenly Father to take care of you. Ask Him for protection from whatever is making you afraid. You might also talk to a big person whom you know you can trust, about your fears and concerns. And remember, your Heavenly Father is bigger and stronger than anyone or anything, and He cares about you.

Why is it wrong if I betray a confidence?

My friend told me something interesting about her family, but then asked me not to share it with anybody. But it was so interesting that I did share it with somebody else. Now my friend is mad at me.

Here is what the Bible says:

"Don't betray another person's secret. Others may accuse you of gossip and you will never regain your good reputation." (Proverbs 25:9-10)

Careless gossip can do a lot of damage. It can be hurtful and cause trouble to the other person and can do you a lot of harm too, because people may lose trust in you as a friend and as someone with whom they can share things.

What's wrong with using swear words?

OK! I said a swear word. I used God's Name. So what? Everyone does that. They do it on TV and in movies all the time. It's just a way of talking.

Here is what the Bible says:

"Don't use foul or abusive language. Let everything you say be good and helpful, so that your words will be an encouragement to those who hear them." (Ephesians 4:29)

"Do not misuse the name of the Lord your God. The Lord will not let you go unpunished if you misuse his name." (Exodus 20:7)

Taking the Lord's Name in vain…swearing…makes God unhappy with you. In doing so, you are not showing Him the respect He deserves. And you are setting a bad example to those who see you as a Christian. Be careful what you say!

What's wrong with telling a dirty joke if it's funny?

I like making people laugh.
Doesn't God have a sense of humor?

Here is what the Bible says:

"Obscene stories, foolish talk, and coarse jokes—these are not for you. Instead, let there be thankfulness to God...Don't be fooled by those who try to excuse their sins, for the terrible anger of God will fall on all who disobey Him." (Ephesians 5:4,6)

What's wrong with stealing?

If I can use the brain God gave me to take something from a person without their knowing it, isn't that just being smart?

Here is what the Bible says:

"You must not steal." (Exodus 20:15)

"Don't fool yourselves. Those who...are thieves, or greedy people...or cheat people... none of these will have a share in the Kingdom of God."
(1 Corinthians 6:10)

Which is better? To have something you want right now or to have a home in Heaven forever? If you have stolen something, first ask God to forgive you. Say "sorry" and really mean it in your heart. Then go to the person from whom you stole and make things right with them.

Why did Jesus come to earth?
And how can I be sure I will go to Heaven with Him when I die?

God sent His Son Jesus to earth to show people who had forgotten God's Commandments how to obey them. But most people didn't believe He was God's Son and refused to listen to Him. So, just as your parents love you but have to punish you when you've done wrong, God could not let disobedient people come and live in Heaven with Him. But not having us in Heaven with Him made God sad, so He allowed His Son Jesus to take the punishment we should have had. All we have to do is tell God we are sorry for sinning and thank Jesus for taking our punishment, and we are forgiven! But those who refuse to ask for forgiveness or who turn their back on Jesus will never be in Heaven and never have eternal life.

Here is what the Bible says:

"For this is how God loved the world: He gave His one and only Son, so that everyone who believes in him will not perish but have eternal life."
(John 3:16)

What Jesus said to His followers as He was preparing to return to Heaven, He says to you too:

"Don't let your hearts be troubled. Trust in God, and trust also in me. There is more than enough room in my Father's home…I am going to prepare a place for you." (John 14:1-2)

"Anyone who believes in God's Son has eternal life." (John 3:36)

How can I ask God to let me become part of His family
and live in Heaven with Him someday?
What can I say in my prayer?"

Here is what you can say in your prayer:

Dear God,
I'm sorry for all the times I have disobeyed your Commandments. Please forgive me and make me a part of your family. Thank you for sending your only Son Jesus to earth so that my sins could be forgiven and so that I can come to live in Heaven with You for ever and ever. Amen.

What if I do bad things?

I thanked God for sending Jesus
and forgiving my sins,
and for making me His child,
but then I did some bad things
that probably made God sad.
Will He forgive me if I say I'm sorry
and really mean it?
Will He still let me be His child?"

Here is what the Bible says:

"If we confess our sins to him, he is faithful and just to forgive us our sins and to cleanse us from all wickedness." (1 John 1:9)

King David of Israel tried to please God every day, but even he failed and had to ask for forgiveness. Here is what he wrote about it:

"Finally, I confessed all my sins to you, and stopped trying to hide my guilt. I said to myself, 'I will confess my rebellion to the Lord.' And you forgave me! All my guilt is gone." (Psalm 32:5)

Nobody is perfect! Try as hard as we can, we will make mistakes in judgment, and do or say things God wouldn't want us to do or say. Does that mean that God is going to give up on you? Of course not! All God wants is to hear you say "sorry" and really mean it, and He will forgive you. And remember, just as God forgives you when you really mean it, He wants you to forgive others who have been mean to you or done something you didn't like. He wants you to be just like Him.

Why did God create me?
What does He want me to do?
Am I of any use to God
or anyone?
People tell me that I'm stupid,
or that I have nothing
important to say.

God has created you and put you in His world to do an important job for Him. He gives each of us special talents to do these jobs. He will help you discover them if you ask Him. Maybe He has given you a heart of love for the poor and homeless, and you will serve Him by giving them food and clothing or someday even a place in your home. Maybe He has given you musical talent to brighten the lives of the lonely and depressed by playing piano or guitar for them or singing in a choir. Maybe He has given you the ability to manage well the money He gives you, and you will be able to help pay the expenses of people serving God in various ways. Maybe He has given you the ability to teach the Bible clearly, and you will become a pastor or hold Bible studies in your home, or He has given you the ability to learn other languages easily and you will serve Him as a missionary. Maybe God has given you great athletic ability so that you can show the world what it means to be a Christian athlete. Or maybe God has given you the talent of being a good listener and prayer warrior, so that when people share their troubles and hopes with you and you say, "I will pray for you," they know you will.

Final Words

The Bible verses quoted in this little book are just a sample of the good advice you will find in the Bible. I encourage you to read it every day. And  don't just read it once! When you are done reading it, go back and start all over again. I promise that you will learn new things every time you read it, and they will help you all through your life. God doesn't promise that your life will be without troubles and difficulties, but He does promise to help you get through them. He wants you to become the person He designed you to be, so that you can do wonderful work for Him. And be on the lookout for God's enemy, Satan. He will do his best to lead you away from God's path for you. He will send people and thoughts to try and discourage you, to make you feel that you can't do anything right or that you're not as smart as other people or that the work you are doing for God is of no value. Don't listen to him! What God said to the people of Israel He says to you too:

"Do not be afraid, for I have ransomed you. I have called you by name; you are mine. When you go through deep waters, I will be with you."
(Isaiah 43:1-2)

"'For I know the plans I have for you,' says the Lord. 'They are plans for good and not for disaster, to give you a future and a hope.'" (Jeremiah 29:11)

Don't miss out on the life God has planned for you! Work at staying close to Him. When you do find yourself wandering away, come right back! Ask Him for forgiveness, and He will forgive you. He is always there to listen to your prayers. I pray you will find His path for your life and never leave it.

Acknowledgements

Many thanks to Janet Weiler at Wheatley Baptist Church, for getting me moving on this project; to my husband Norm, for putting up with all the hours I was "holed up" in my office with it; to my tech guy Kevin and James R. Coggins for their long-suffering with my lack of computer knowledge; to my son Scott, for helping me get the project sent off in the correct form; and to my best friend Doreen, for always believing in and encouraging me.

www.ingramcontent.com/pod-product-compliance
Lightning Source LLC
Chambersburg PA
CBHW081015120626
46546CB00010B/3157